Healthy Eating

Bread Rice and Pasta

Susan Martineau and Hel James

W

FRANKLIN WATTS

LONDON•SYDNEY

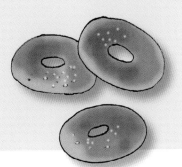

An Appleseed Editions book

First published in 2006 by
Franklin Watts
338 Euston Road
London NW1 3BH

Franklin Watts Australia
Hachette Children's Books
Level 17/207 Kent Street
Sydney NSW 2000

© 2006 Appleseed Editions

Created by Appleseed Editions Ltd,
Well House, Friars Hill, Guestling, East Sussex TN35 4ET

Designed and illustrated by Helen James
Edited by Jinny Johnson

ISBN-10: 0-7496-6724-9
ISBN-13: 978-0-7496-6724-5
Dewey Classification: 641.3

A CIP catalogue for this book is available from the British Library

Photographs: 10-11 James Marshall/Corbis; 12-13 Susan Martineau; 16 PhotoCuisine/Corbis; 18-19 Tom Bean/Corbis; 21 Charles Gupton/Corbis; 25 Vittoriano Rastelli/Corbis; 29 Michael Freeman/Corbis. Front cover: James Noble/Corbis

Printed and bound in Thailand

Contents

Food for health

Our bodies are like amazing machines.
Just like machines, we need the right
sort of fuel to give us energy and
to keep us working properly.

If we don't eat the kind of food
we need to keep us healthy we
may become ill or feel tired and
grumpy. Our bodies don't really
like it if we eat too much of one
sort of food, like cakes or chips.

We need a balanced diet.
That means eating different
sorts of good food in the
right amounts.

You'll be surprised at how much
there is to know about where our
food comes from and why some
kinds of food are better for us
than others. Finding out about
food is great fun and very tasty!

I'm really hungry.

A balanced plateful!

The good things or nutrients our bodies need come from different kinds of food. Let's have a look at what your plate should have on it. It all looks delicious!

Rice, bread and pasta

These foods contain carbohydrates and they give us energy. They are also called starchy foods. About a third of your food should come from this group.

Fruit and vegetables

Rice, bread and pasta

Chicken with rice and vegetables is a great balanced plateful.

6

Fruit and vegetables

These are full of great vitamins and minerals and fibre. They do all kinds of useful jobs in your body to help keep you healthy. About a third of our food should come from this group.

Meat, fish and eggs

Protein from these helps your body grow and repair itself. They are body-building foods and you need to eat some of them every day.

Milk, yogurt and cheese

These dairy foods give us protein and also calcium to make strong bones and teeth.

Sugar and fats

We only need small amounts of these. Too much can be bad for our teeth and make us fat.

Milk, yogurt and cheese

Sugar and fats

Meat, fish and eggs

Water

We need to drink at least 6 glasses of water every day.

7

Energy foods

Try to eat a portion of energy food at every meal. You could work out a super-charged menu for the day with lots of energy foods.

Super-charged menu

Breakfast

A big bowl of cereal with fruit or a bowl of porridge oats make a very good breakfast.

Rice, bread and pasta are our main power-packed foods. Some other foods like breakfast cereals and potatoes give us energy too.

Breakfast is a great start to the day.

Super-charged menu
Lunch

Enjoy a sandwich or roll with your favourite filling.

Did you know you use up energy even when you're sitting down?

Facts

Super-charged menu
Dinner

Eat a dish of pasta, noodles or rice with tasty vegetables or meat.

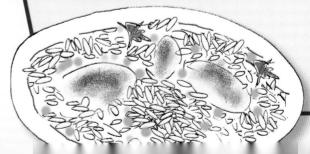

A bowl of rice

Rice grains are the seeds of the rice plant. It is a cereal plant, like wheat, oats or barley.

Rice grows in many parts of the world, but most comes from Asia, America and Australia. The rice plants grow best when their roots are under water. That's why rice fields, or paddy fields, are very wet places.

In Asia the rice plants are planted in the fields by hand. In America and Australia the rice seeds are dropped by aeroplane.

Ancient food

In Asia rice has been grown and eaten for 5000 years. In places like China and India people often eat rice two or three times a day.

Harvesting rice

When the rice has grown and is ready to be harvested it is cut by hand or by huge machines called combine harvesters. The rice grains then have to be separated from the stalks.

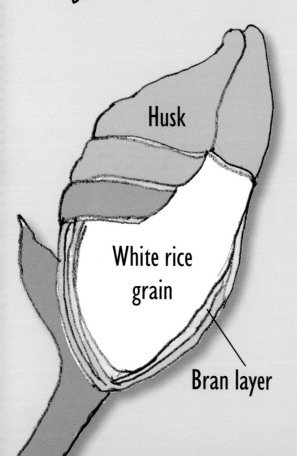

Brown rice

Husk

White rice grain

Bran layer

Hard husks on the outside of the grain are taken off to make the rice ready for us to eat. This leaves a layer of bran on the grain and gives us brown rice. Bran is really good for you as it contains vitamins and fibre.

But this bran layer is usually removed to make the white rice we have all seen in the shops. White rice is still a very good energy food, but brown rice is better for us.

White rice

In Asia the grains and stalks are separated by hand. In America and Australia this is done by machines.

Know your rice!

Rice is used in many delicious dishes around the world. It can be eaten hot or cold, in sweet or savoury foods. There are three main types of rice: long grain, medium grain and short grain.

Basmati is a long-grain rice used in Indian cookery. The grains don't stick together when they are cooked. Basmati is great with curries.

Arborio is a medium-grain rice. It is used in a tasty Italian dish called risotto.

Try cooking some rice yourself, but ask an adult to help.

Short-grain rice goes nice and sticky when it is cooked so it's good for rice pudding.

Rice spotter

Next time you are in a food shop or supermarket, see how many types of rice you can spot! Which ones have you tried eating?

Breakfast boost

Rice grains are made into breakfast food by puffing them up. Other grains from cereal plants, like oats, barley and wheat, are also used to make breakfast cereals. Corn flakes are made from maize. Extra vitamins, minerals and iron are added to breakfast cereals to make them even better for you.

Cereal, milk and fruit make a nutrient-packed start to your day.

The best breakfast cereals are the ones made with whole grains or wheat. Look out for the words 'wholegrain' or 'wholewheat' on the cereal packet.

Sugar alert

There's a lot of sugar in some breakfast cereals. Have a look at the list of ingredients. If sugar is near the top of the list, choose another kind of cereal. Too much sugar is bad for your teeth!

Bring on the bread

Bread is made from flour and water. Flour is made by grinding up the grains from cereal plants. Most of the bread we eat is made from wheat flour. Flour can also be made from maize, rye or oats.

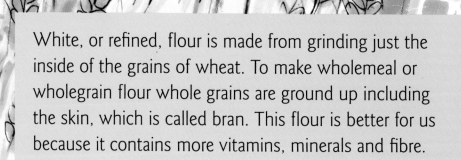

White, or refined, flour is made from grinding just the inside of the grains of wheat. To make wholemeal or wholegrain flour whole grains are ground up including the skin, which is called bran. This flour is better for us because it contains more vitamins, minerals and fibre.

The grain is harvested using massive machines called combine harvesters.

Wheat grain

Inside of the grain

Bran

Making bread

Some people make their own bread at home, but most of us buy bread from a bakery or supermarket. This bread is made in factory bakeries by huge machines.

Flour, water, salt and yeast are measured into enormous tubs and mixed together to make dough. The dough is cut into pieces and put into tins. It is left for a time while the yeast makes it 'rise' or get bigger. Then it is put into a giant oven to be baked.

Some of the loaves are kept whole and some are sliced before being put into packaging and sent off to the shops.

Mix flour, water and yeast to make dough.

Knead the dough, then put it in a bowl and leave it to rise.

Eat it up!

Bread doesn't keep for very long and is best eaten when it is fresh. Dates on labels tell you how soon the bread should be eaten.

Put the dough in a tin.

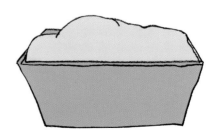

Bake it in the oven.

A world of bread

There are so many delicious breads to choose from. Next time you go shopping, have a look at some different kinds and maybe choose a new one to try. Bread can be eaten with all sorts of meals.

This one's wholemeal!

Wholemeal loaves and rolls

These are really good for you, but check the labels for the words wholemeal, wholewheat or wholegrain. Then you know it's the best of brown bread!

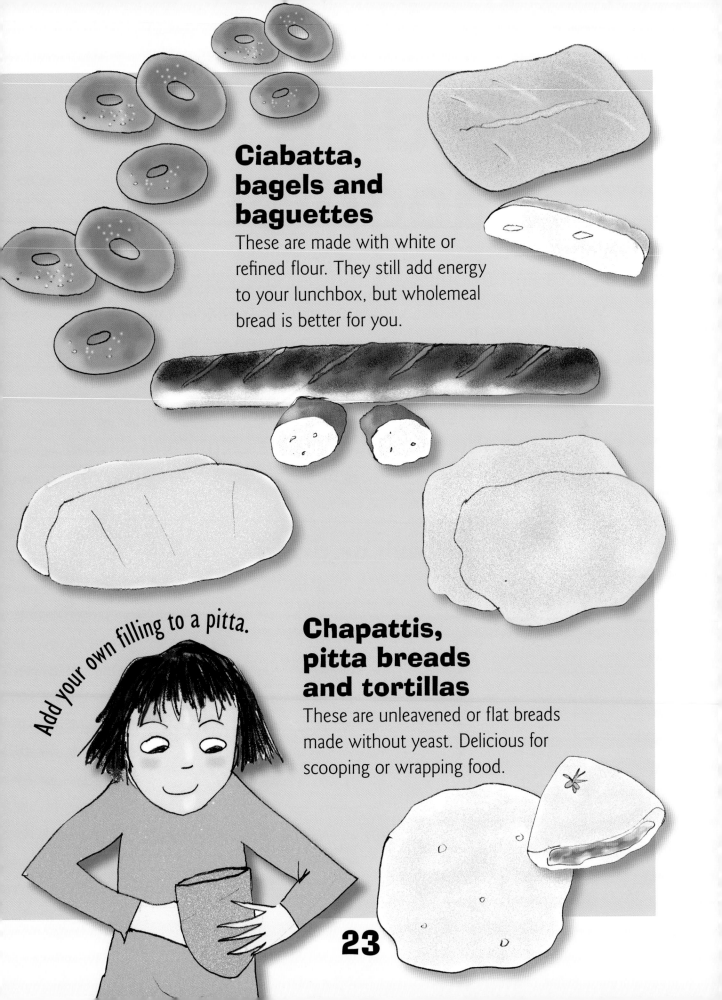

Ciabatta, bagels and baguettes

These are made with white or refined flour. They still add energy to your lunchbox, but wholemeal bread is better for you.

Add your own filling to a pitta.

Chapattis, pitta breads and tortillas

These are unleavened or flat breads made without yeast. Delicious for scooping or wrapping food.

23

Oodles of noodles

Pasta and noodles are another energy-packed food which is eaten all over the world. Italian-style pasta is made from wheat flour and water. Pasta, like bread, can be made with wholemeal or white flour. Sometimes egg or oil is mixed in too. Tomato or spinach can also be added for extra colour and flavour.

Fresh or dried?

You can buy fresh or dried pasta. Fresh pasta does not keep for long. Dried pasta can keep for up to two years!

SNAP!

Fresh pasta is soft and floppy, dried pasta is hard and brittle.

The dried pasta shapes you see in the shops are made in factories.

In the pasta factories, flour and water are made into dough in huge tubs. Then the dough is shaped to make different types of pasta, dried and put into bags or packages.

Piles of pasta

Did you know that there are more than 600 different pasta shapes? You won't find all of them in your local shop, but you could have some fun seeing how many kinds you can spot.

Pasta provides us with carbohydrate. When it is served with some meat or vegetable sauce it makes just the sort of balanced plateful our bodies like.

Tasty parcels

These tubes or packages of pasta contain tasty mixtures of meat, cheese and vegetables.

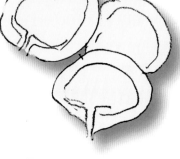
Tortelloni

Ravioli

Cannelloni

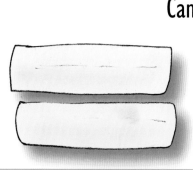

Fun shapes

Even the names of these are fun.

Penne — quills

Farfalle — butterflies
or bow-ties

Fusilli — spirals

Conchiglie — shells

Long and thin

Munch these with your favourite meat or
vegetable sauce or just sprinkle
some cheese on top.

Linguine

Tagliatelle

Spaghetti

Oriental noodles

Asian-style noodles are also made from wheat flour and water. Sometimes egg is added to make delicious yellow egg noodles. Noodles can be made with other types of flour too. Rice noodles are made from rice flour and cellophane noodles from ground-up mung beans.

SLURP!

In Asia you can buy these noodles all freshly made. In other places, you can buy them dried, in packets. They can all be made into great nutritious meals.

Noodle soups and stir-fries are a healthy plateful. Choose your favourite vegetables, fish or meat and add them to noodle soup or stir-fried noodles. Then slurp them up!

How
many
different
sorts of
noodles
can you
see?

Words to remember

bran   The thin, brown layer underneath the husks of cereal grains. Bran contains iron and B vitamins.

calcium   A mineral that helps build healthy bones and teeth. Dairy foods are high in calcium.

carbohydrates   The starches and sugars in food that give us energy. Rice, pasta, bread and potatoes are all carbohydrate foods.

cereals   These are types of grass plants grown for food. Examples are wheat, rice, rye, maize, barley, oats and millet.

dairy foods   Foods made from milk, such as cheese, butter, cream and yogurt.

dough   A soft, thick mixture made of flour and water.

factory bakeries   Bread is made in very large quantities in these bakeries to supply supermarkets and shops.

fibre   This is found in plant foods like grains and vegetables. It helps our insides to work properly.

harvested   When crops are cut down and gathered for food.

iron   A mineral in food that we need to keep our blood healthy.

minerals   Nutrients in food that help our bodies work properly. Calcium and iron are minerals.

nutrients   Parts of food that your body needs for energy, to grow healthily and to repair itself.

nutritious   Containing lots of nutrients.

protein   Body-building food that makes our bodies grow well and stay healthy.

wholegrain/wholemeal/wholewheat   Bread and cereals made using the whole grains of cereal plants like wheat.

unleavened   Bread made without using yeast to make it rise.

vitamins   Nutrients in food which help our bodies work properly. The B vitamins in bran help to turn our food into energy and also help our muscles, skin and blood.

yeast   Yeast is added to dough to make it puff up and make bread with bubbles in it.

Index

WEBSITES

General food information for all ages
www.bbc.co.uk/health/healthy_living/nutrition

Food Standards Agency – healthy eating,
food labelling
www.eatwell.gov.uk

Quizzes and games on food
www.coolfoodplanet.org

Information and games on healthy eating
www.lifebytes.gov.uk/eating/eat_menu.html

Worksheets and activities
www.foodforum.org.uk

Practical advice on healthy eating
www.fitness.org.uk